PRINTED WOR]

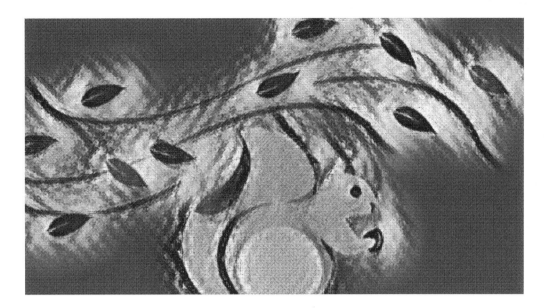

AUTUMN 2019

ISSUE 3

Welcome to our third issue of Printed Words. We have poetry and fiction with a book review thrown in, for you to read and hopefully enjoy. I owe an apology to Zoë Sîobhan Howarth-Lowe. Due to human-error (mine) her poem "Grandmother" wasn't included in full last time. You can read the full version in this issue instead.

We had so many amazing writers in our last magazine that our judge couldn't pick just one winner. Therefore, Sarra Culleno and Randall Horton shared the prize. Congratulations, to both of you.

By the time this goes to print, we will have attended our first festival as a publication. You should be able to see the photos and videos on our Facebook page.

Please follow us on Facebook for updates.
www.facebook.com/PrintedWordsEzine

Amanda Steel (Editor)

Amanda Steel
(Editor and Submissions Reader)
Amanda Steel is the author of the YA novel *First Charge* and has just released a poetry collection called *Pieces of Me*.
Amanda also co-hosts the podcast *Reading in Bed* and sometimes she writes under the pen name *Aleesha Black*.
Her website is www.amandasteelwriter.com

Andy N
(Submissions Reader)
Andy N is the author of three poetry collections, the most recent being *The Birth of Autumn*. He also co-runs *Speak Easy*, Stretford's leading poetry open mic, and runs/co-runs the podcast series *Spoken Label* and *Reading in Bed*, on top of regularly doing ambient music under the name *Ocean in a Bottle*
https://onewriterandhispc.blogspot.com/

Steve Smythe
(Judge)
Steve Smythe juggles his job as a car park specialist with his creative writing. He co-runs *Speak Easy* with Andy N. Steve writes poetry and flash fiction and enjoys letting his real life influence his fiction, so that you never can tell where the lines blur.
You can find him on Twitter.
https://twitter.com/smooth2go

Sarra Culleno
(Guest Submissions Reader)
Sarra Culleno is a London born, Manchester based English teacher and mother of two, who writes and performs both formal and free-verse poetry on identity, motherhood, age, modern monogamy, technology, the education system — and so much more.
She regularly performs at open mics around Manchester and recently came second in The Poetry Café's Easter Slam in Convent Garden.
www.facebook.com/sarracullenopoetry/

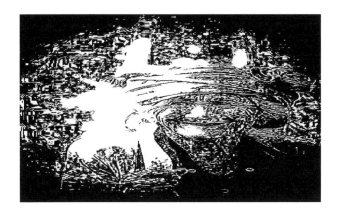

Grandmother
By Zoe Sîobhan Howarth-Lowe

1.
Walking downstairs late at night,
I find the front room door open
and there she is.

Sat in her favourite armchair.
A cigarette in her fingers,
her face turned away from me.

I turn, head out into the garden,
staring upwards
seeking Orion flexing his bow,
but I stumble,

and there she is again.
Sat in her favourite sun-lounger,
covered by a blanket
that lifts a little as I rise to my feet

and I see her hand,
still clutching the cigarette.

2.
The telephone wakes me from sleep.
I hear my mother's voice in her bedroom,
talking quickly and high pitched.
The phone clicks against the cradle
and my mother's door clicks open.
She is walking towards me,
coming to explain.
I try to tell her that I already know.

3.
The family gathers outside a church,
every cheek I kiss is thick with salt,
thick enough to taste.
I want it out of me;
vomiting on the church steps,
I leave the salt for slugs to feast on.
Hoping I can stay to watch
as they boil inside their own skins.

4.
She is in a box,
and I am trapped in a room of sniffs.

She is in a box,
and I am waiting for them to open it.

She is in a box,
and I am waiting for her to sit up,
swear at us for locking her in
and knock the ash off her cigarette.

She is in that box,
and I do not want to get any closer,
but someone is pushing me,
jostling me towards the polished wood,
and I notice the nails.

She is in a box,
and she is nailed in.

Author Bio
Zoë is a Poet and Mum from Dukinfield. She has an MA in Poetry from Bath Spa
University.
Her first pamphlet 'Love is the way bark grows' comes out with Half Moon Books in
June 2019.
Her work has appeared in Anthologies and Journals including For the Silent, Atrium,
Ink, Sweat and Tears, Picaroon, Algebra of Owls, Bonnie's Crew and Marble.
Website: https://zshowarth-lowe.weebly.com/

Winter Years
By Chris Neilson

Spring years bring education
preparation, joy and jubilation
blooming teenage angst too
tearing at fragile egos and acne
but largely in good health
if not wealth or privilege
a decade of decadence
with nascent or no common sense

Summer years in prime time
roaring twenties and flirty thirties
seduction and reproduction
too busy to worry as you scurry
climbing ladders of opportunity
or confidently batting away stress
but occasionally making a mess
as we're human after all

Ah the fearful Autumn years
declining health spent scrabbling
cupboards filled with medication
Doctors finding inventive new ways
to keep us alive with sticks and chairs
you may be lucky in greying gracefully
an occasional old swinger in town
all your marbles present and correct

Winter years are those we experience
at any forsaken time in our lives
where problems mount without warning
freezing the assets we lived by
icily gripped by fear, teary and weary
but all cold snaps do inevitably end
riding out the storm can seem forlorn
but the blackbird will sing again in spring

Author Bio
After dropping out of college, Chris Neilson embarked upon a working life of toil in a variety of mostly spirit crushing employment, then accepted voluntary redundancy in 2012.
The English language has always been his academic strong point, but writing had been an unexplored well, so with his new-found freedom he made the radical decision to evolve into a part time postal worker and part time poet.
Chris states that he has never had any formal creative writing training. His mainly rhythmic, lyrical material is organic and covers a wide range of subjects emanating from deep within his soul.
https://twitter.com/MancMinstrel

Longford Theatre
By Andy N

To me, it's always been
a ghostly shell of the past
rotting on the side of Chester Road
for more years
than I can remember
but my father remembers it differently.

He remembers it being described
as a high-class place
which featured shows
by the Halle Orchestra
after they got bombed out of Manchester
during the Second World War.

I only remember it as a run
down bingo hall with assistants
who clearly were more interested
in polishing their fingernails
than working there
but my father remembers it differently.

He remembers being told
back when he was a child
the building was the first in Britain
to be illuminated
by neon tube lighting.

He remembers being told
the foyer was floored in Venetian Marble
and the auditorium
was decorated in tangerine
with silver-blue art-deco
and still lists off with pride
the major stars he saw there
during their Sunday shows
when he was growing up
just after the war.

He remembers the internal decoration
being done by Holdings of Brooks Bar
that included as a centre-piece of
two huge murals
that were on either side
of the main stage
one of which stated in colourful letters
'Music and Dance'
in contrast on the other which stated
'Comedy and Drama'.

He remembers being told
it was opened on 12th October 1936
by the Mayor of Stretford
Alderman Albert Smith
and his father going to watch
the first film screened there
'Tudor Rose'
starring Nova Pilbeam.

To me however it's always been
a ghostly shell of the past
rotting on the side of Chester Road
that last became
a dodgy Bingo hall
briefly before shutting again
even though the rumours
of it re-opening are still ongoing.

Even though my father
remembers it differently.

(Note from Andy – Longford Theatre
can be found on the corner of Chester Road
opposite Stretford Arndale, Stretford, Manchester)

Sold Out
By Anthony Briscoe

I feel like chicken tonight
Chicken Tonight
Chicken Tonight

I just don't feel right
And I know I'm feeling weaker when I really should be stronger, but I'm not powered by
Duracell the battery, that's the battery that lasts longer

You see, there's a saying that you should take the smooth with the rough but I'm not the
Milky Bar kid, he's strong and tough and only the best is good enough the creamiest
milk, the whitest bar the good taste that's in Milky Bar!

Maybe I should man up
Grab a Snickers, get some nuts

But my heart feels broken like a Yorkie bar that's dropped to the ground, that's not well
sold to girls

You see a relationship that slowly fades and dies over time cannot simply Shake and Vac
to put the freshness back

Although I keep jumping through hoops like giant Polos, the mint with the hole

And I don't know what to do and you only get an "oo" with Typhoo

So I'm planting my seeds of hope into lines and hoping those beans of hope flourish and
remember beans means Heinz

My friends are saying to me, *Ant slow down your going too fast you're trying too hard,
there's always alternatives.* And they are right because for everything else there's
Mastercard

And it's all because the lady loves Milk Tray

But not me

Maybe I should just have a break --- have a Kit Kat

But oh, oh TWO we are better connected

That I believe and I have no uncertain T--Mobile life is for sharing

But love is something deep inside like a Subway sandwich that I want to eat fresh

She had the most beautiful eyes I have ever seen, maybe she's born with it, maybe it's Maybelline

And I wanted those eyes to fall upon me, so me and her could just restart this but I feel like I'm missing something, that Max Factor, the makeup of makeup artists

And I wish I could say my name is Ron---seal - exactly what it says on the tin

Or John Smith's - no nonsense

But I can't do any of that because my brain is mashed and remember for mash eat Smash

But she was so good like Cravendale milk, EVEN THE COWS WANT IT BACK!!!

And is you saw her, you would say she had this kind of Kia-Ora which is too orangey for crows and everybody knows when you see her out and about, her beauty hits you like COVONIA cough medicine with clout

She had the most beautifully built body that I had ever seen, she also did have the temperament of a queen and she would only eat only the most healthy prepared cuisine - I suppose you could say she was a lean mean fat reducing grilling machine

But I don't have that, I am now on my own

And no Mars a day helps you work rest and play

And happiness is not a cigar called hamlet

And even though Heineken refreshes the other parts that beers cannot reach, the answers are not at the bottom of a bottle

You have to get up every day and go to work on an egg

Take each day and Nike n just do it!

And try to forget holding her hands that do dishes that felt as soft as your face when you use mild green Fairy Liquid

And how I would just Flake apart like only the crumbliest flakiest chocolate like chocolate has never tasted before

And I need to pick myself up like I would p-p-p-p-pick up a Penguin

Because I know that I've been Tango'd

I feel like Aldi like brands but only cheaper

And I remain upset and cry evidently, but at least I can dry my tears and use ONE SHEET, that does Plenty!

And I'll try and reinvent myself and do it by the book and try to get the London look

Because the future's bright the futures Orange but it's not Terry's ITS MINE!!

And I shall throw away my worries and live like Sainsbury's and live well for less and everyone I know and everyone I love will become my Tesco's, because every little helps

And I will explain myself like I always do like I always do - ORAL - B the number one recommended by dentists

And not resent myself when alone at night because love it or hate it - that's Marmite

I shall do all this but never fully forget that she was my GILLETTE THE BEST A MAN CAN GET

And for while throughout everything I thought she was my one and although I do not know where we went wrong, I thought she was my one but maybe, just maybe I need to accept she's
WASHING MACHINES LAST LONGER WITH CALGON….

Author Bio
Anthony Briscoe is a performance poet and freelance artist from Blackpool, currently living in Manchester. His Poetry ranges from political social commentary, space, advertisements replacing love and even clowns. Anthony likes to mix the serious and the silly to discuss meaningful issues through an absurdist lens, using his background in theatrics to add an energetic, engaging and entertaining performance to all his material. He was recently a guest on Spoken Label
https://spokenlabel.bandcamp.com/album/ant-briscoe-spoken-label-july-2019

Jimmy Smith Has a Dinosaur
By Gregg Chamberlain
(Previously appeared in Daily Science Fiction – March 2013.)

"Moooooommmmmm! Pleeeeease?"

"No, Billy, you can't have one."

Billy's mom picked up another plate, one of the chipped ones, and started wiping it dry with quick, almost-savage strokes of the dishtowel. She knew what was coming next.

"But why, mom?" argued Billy. "Jimmy Smith has a dinosaur!"

Billy's mom sighed. Put the plate in the cupboard, reached for another, began wiping it dry. "If Jimmy Smith's parents choose to let him have a dinosaur, that is their decision and they can afford to do so. Me, I really don't think it's proper to let a child have that kind of a pet."

Even if it is "just a micro-sized plant-eater" like Amelia said.

"But moooooommmmmm!"

"Don't 'but mom!' me!" Billy's mom spat. "No dinosaur and that is final!"

Billy scuffed a sneaker-clad foot against a crack in the kitchen linoleum. "S'not fair. Jimmy Smith gets to have a dinosaur, he gets to ride around on his own SeaSkidoo, gets to learn kickboxing with Jackie Chan's clone, go to Mars for summer holidays, to…"

"Oh, for pity's sake!" Billy's mom cried in exasperation. "If Jimmy Smith got permission to jump off a cliff, would you want to go too?"

Blessed silence followed. For a moment. Then…

"Jimmy Smith has a jetpack."

Author Bio

Gregg Chamberlain is A community newspaper reporter, living in rural Ontario, Canada, with his missus, Anne, and their clowder of cats, who allow the humans to believe they are in charge. He has several dozen pieces of short fiction in various magazines and original anthologies.

Summary in Free Verse
By Anne Mikusinski

Music in rehearsal
Muffled but still raw
Pulses through the
Closed steel door
I stand outside
Listening
As anticipation
Makes its first appearance.

Later
An unexpected meeting
Carbonated anxiety
And giddiness
All mixed in
First impressions
On a cloudy evening.

During
No sense of time exists
Just community
Words and music
The poetry
Of pure expression.

Author Bio
Anne Mikusinski has been writing poems since she was seven years old and probably making them up long before that. She loves words, the way they fit together and how they can make the reader feel things.
Her influences range from Dylan Thomas and Sylvia Plath to David Byrne and Nick Cave. Anne hope that someday, her own writing will be as much as an influence on someone as these writers have been for her.

A Broken-Down Journey of Grief
By Amber Kaysen

The car careened off the road
The driver saw the warning sign
Signalling fuel was low
But never really believed it
Until it was empty

That's when denial took over
It sat behind the wheel
Mimicking the growl of an engine
Pretending to swerve from left to right
As though the car was still on the road

Guilt snatched the wheel away
And blamed itself for not seeing
For refusing to believe
For not driving faster
For everything it could think of

Bargaining slapped its hands
Against the wheel
Thinking of everything it would take back
Of everything it should have done or said
It would do or say it all now, if only

Depression took over when bargaining failed
When guilt became too overbearing
Then reality proved denial wrong
And shock turned to belief
Leaving nothing left to do

Until a better day arrived
And acceptance set in
But the car was still broken down
By the side of the forest
And they all walked a lonely road

Sometimes denial still pretends to drive
And guilt hits without warning
While bargains are never found
Leading to long visits from depression
Before acceptance holds out it's hand again

The Unwanted Present
By Amber Kaysen

Pretty little lies
Wrapped up with a fancy bow
Like a gift I never asked for
Cancelling out all the words
That came before the present
And I try to give it back
But those words are out there now
And I'll never know the difference
Between truth and lies
Mistaken kindness and genuine praise

Author Bio
Amber Kaysen is a Canadian poet. She has just released "I See Myself in the Distance",
a pamphlet of brutally honest poetry which some readers may find upsetting.
https://www.amazon.ca/See-Myself-Distance-Amber-Kaysen/dp/1079723218

Empty Halls
By Pete Slater

Standing on
The ledge
Standing at the edge
Of tomorrow
No time to waste
No time for
Sorrow
We only get a taste
Of eternity
We have to embrace
Diversity
Or like a flickering
Flame
This fragile game
Of life
Will suffocate
And die
Leaving only
Empty halls
Inhabited by
Ghosts

And graffiti scarred
Walls
Showing man
Was ever
Here
At
All.

Author Bio

Pete describes himself as an accidental poet who finds poetry cathartic, a great release for happiness, sadness, love and hate all in equal measure. He has a Facebook page … "Pete Slater Poet" and a similarly titled you tube channel where you can find audio-visual attempts to purvey his "poetry" He is a great advocator of multimedia presentation, but wishes he was more tech minded.
https://www.youtube.com/user/Petenbern

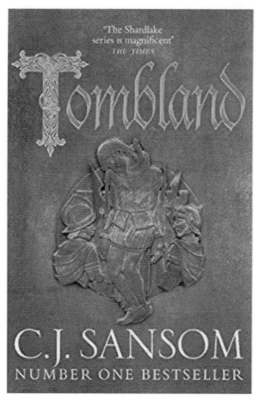

Review of Tombland - CJ Sansom
(ISBN 978-1447284482)
Reviewed by Derek McMillan

"Tombland" is the latest in the Shardlake series by C.J. Sansom. It is a murder mystery set in the 16th Century. There are no spoilers in this review about who the murderer was. However, the story is set against the real historical background of the Kett rebellion.

In the reign of Edward VI (when real power resided with his uncle, the Duke of Somerset who reigned in his name) the gentry and yeoman farmers had taken to enclosing land and giving it over to sheep. They forced small farmers off the land which was also given over to sheep production. Not only did the people lose the use of common land for their own sheep, but agriculture was devastated.

As a result of a disastrous war with Scotland and the debasement of the currency, prices rose out of control while wages stagnated.

One Norfolk yeoman farmer, Robert Kett, was approached by rebellious commoners who demanded he remove the enclosures he had made. Not only did he do so but he ended up leading the rebellion in Norfolk, which became the largest of its kind in the country.

An estimated force of 16000 rebels set up a massive camp on Mousehold Heath, to the North of Norwich. Under Kett's leadership, the rebels stormed Norwich and took the city. The workers in the city sympathised with the rebels and assisted the takeover. The forces of the aristocracy thought the rebels would be a walkover and sent an army against them under the Marquess of Northampton. He was comprehensively defeated.

The rebels however had faith that the government genuinely intended to deliver on its promise to end illegal enclosures. That is a bit like expecting the 1 percent to act in the interests of the 99 percent. Instead, the King's army under the Earl of Warwick was sent to massacre the rebels with the aid of 1200 mercenaries.

The story is a useful antidote to books and TV series about the pomp and ceremony of the Tudor court and the intrigues of the aristocracy. The flip side of that coin was the unimaginable brutality with which aristocrats like Warwick treated the commoners. He only stopped because the gentlemen did not fancy putting their own hands to the plough, so repentant commoners were spared.

Even a book about the 16th Century has a valuable lesson. Not only does it show the power of the common people to fight for justice, but also the perfidious nature of the upper classes.

Author Bio
Derek McMillan is a writer based in Durrington-on-sea. His wife, Angela, is his editor. He has written short stories for a number of magazines. Derek runs a blog for flash fiction.
http://worthingflash.blogspot.com

Cross That Bridge When You Get to It
By Amanda Steel

The only people to live nearby were afraid of crossing bridges. This wouldn't be a problem if they lived somewhere less remote. However, they lived in the middle of nowhere and the only way to get to the nearest town was to cross the bridge. All four generations of the family had all been born with Gephyrophobia.

Great Grandmother became ill and the only way to get medicine was to cross the bridge into town. Abbey, the youngest at age ten volunteered to go. After all, she almost crossed the bridge that one time when hunting rabbits in the woods. In her haste to provide meat for the stew, she was halfway across the bridge in pursuit if a huge rabbit before she realised and ran back home. Surely now she could make it all the way across, for her great grandmother's sake.

So, off she went. There were no rabbits around for her to chase this time. She made it to the bridge and stretched out one leg, then the other so that she was standing on it. She told herself this was a simple case of taking one step after the other, but maybe it would help if she couldn't see she on the bridge.

Abbey closed her eyes and continued to take one slow step after another until she finally opened her eyes. She was on a road; the road leading to town. She turned around and couldn't see the way back anywhere. She had walked too far with her eyes close.

I don't know what happened to Abbey's great grandmother, or the rest of her family, but I suppose it there's a moral to this story, it should be that you ought to face your fears with your eyes wide open.

When the Devil Smiles
By Nigel Astell

Frantic pecking hungry birds
frozen seed needs replacing
blizzard conditions, coldness bites
temperature falls below zero
warm heart, numb fingers
survival food lightly scattered
feathered flock gratefully swoop
door closes, locked out
picking up solid stone
throwing hard, sheer panic
glass splinters, bleeding arm
calling out, birds fly
frantic resistance, shivering blue
killer frost, hope freezes
paralyzed limbs, raw surrender
death strikes, devil smiles
stiff white corpse discovered.

***

This was one of the worst Winter Storms Canada ever had.

Twenty-seven people were killed one of them an old lady. She had gone out in her back garden with high walls of snow to feed the poor birds.

A lifeless white body was found the following day, she had been unable to get
inside her house and was so desperate tried to break the glass but all the windows were hardened ice. Soon, so was she.

Author Bio
Nigel is a member of Stockport Write Out Loud Poetry Group. He likes the valuable support of personal friendship which bonds strong positive energy to produce a higher level of enjoyment to his writing. He is known for his explicit poetry. However, he often produces more serious work, usually to the acclaim from the other group members of "you wouldn't expect that from Nigel".
https://www.writeoutloud.net/profiles/nigelastell

Alone in Warsaw
By Mark Edward Jones

I am alone now. Five adults, eight other children and that man. Gone. The planes came again after dinner, sooner than usual. The church had been spared so far, but the bombs found us this time. Each building on our block had its turn, the distant explosions thumping us with their power, followed by a sound like thunder and bright light. Three blasts before our turn, plaster fell from the walls onto the floor of the emptied sanctuary, its pews long ago stripped for firewood. The next flash collapsed the theater across the boulevard, now littered with debris and bodies. The final burst before our turn hit the neighboring parsonage, blowing open our windows and shattering glass over my fellow sufferers.

Then it came. Our bomb. Oh, I know the soldier loading the plane didn't know that particular device would fall on a church. Bombs look the same after all, but each one caused its own mayhem when a house, hospital, doctor's office, or church collapsed, killing those inside. Their hopes and memories lost forever. Our bomb fell on the rear of the sanctuary, striking near the column of marble where my family would sit each Sunday. My father was the best singer…

I awoke near the small kitchen used by the priests, choking on the thick, gray dust filling the sanctuary. It was quieter now, the noise from the bombs far away and growing more distant. The voices of my friends had ceased. The orange glow of fire was all around us, but the church was not burning. There was the night sky where the roof had been, stars blinking through acrid smoke. A moan from far under the rubble. Was everyone else buried? I couldn't remember their names now. They were nice and offered me food after I ran away from those soldiers. Those men took my parents and my brother and tried to get me, but I ran until I came to the church. I thought I would be safe.

Then he came. I saw him push through the smashed Medieval door. A skinny soldier wearing a helmet with that insignia. He was a boy not much older than my brother. I hid in the kitchen, grabbed a butcher knife so large I struggled to keep it upright, and I squeezed behind the splintered pantry. The footsteps stopped and that face shoved itself into my hiding place. I screamed, struggled, and yanked my sleeve away from his grasp, running into the sanctuary where our beds had been. He yelled something I could not understand. I backed into a corner standing in shards of shattered stained glass, and I waited. He found me and smirked that awful smile. I pointed the knife and he laughed, still moving closer. And then … I did it. The blade went smoothly into his gut, and that smile disappeared. He dropped to his knees and fell at my feet. I am alone now.

Author Bio
Mark Edward Jones is a lifelong resident of Oklahoma and a retired administrator in higher education finance. Mark began writing in 2018 after retirement. He submitted an excerpt from his currently untitled novel to The Oklahoma Writers' Federation, Inc. (OWFI), which runs an annual writing contest in several categories for its annual spring convention. This was chosen as "WINNER - 2019 Mystery and Suspense category, OWFI".
In his Henry Ike Pierce series, is the Deep State interfering in a murder investigation or is this just the vivid imagination of a widowed detective?
https://mejbooksllc.com

Evening Walk
By Adrian Slonaker

Viewed along an access road,
celestial zests of azure, violet and buttercream -
as if a blast of blue plum nectar were courting
a bowl of oleo -
compete with a Bennigan's, a Ramada Inn
and an army of headlights heading home.
Stepping cautiously so that my clumsy bare feet
won't trip over the curb, I smirk,
reassured that such sunsets will
survive the obsolescence
of human nonsense and noise.
In the meantime, my right-hand clutches
my room key and a cold convenience-store bottle
of root beer-flavored milk I'd invested ninety-nine cents in
because it reminded me of the floats Nadine, the titian-haired babysitter
with Gloria Vanderbilt jeans and Valley girl inflections,
used to scoop and splash together.
As slivers of lawn - is it Kentucky blue or ryegrass? -
get ironed by my soles, I wonder whether
your bristly brown hair
(like a beaver's fur, but darker),
which you crop yourself to save a few bucks each month,
would feel the same under my fingertips.

The Hermit and the Hippie

By Adrian Slonaker

She focused on him fingering microfilm
at the Minnow Way Community Library,
mesmerized by grainy coupons for milk, long expired
and clips depicting cake walks and
euchre clubs in 1959.
Clad in a charcoal cardigan and tapered tan trousers,
he played the foil for her formless flowing lilac,
olive, and blood orange muslins, mismatched fugitives from a
boho mosh pit.
She beamed affably, flashing a phalanx of crooked teeth.
Nodding with indifference,
he retreated within a terrapin's shell
blackened with bruises, scraped by scratches,
and toughened by time like leather left under a geode.
He bolstered his mistrust of her intrusive warmth with
a megadose of misanthropy
but wasn't made of muscovite mica.
When she coaxed him,
he crawled forth.

Author Bio

Zigzagging back and forth across the Canadian/US border, Adrian Slonaker works as a copywriter and copy editor. Adrian's work has been nominated for *Best of the Net* and has appeared in *Ariel Chart, Aerodrome, WINK: Writers in the Know* and others.

Poem Trapped in Hypercube
By Kealan Coady

When you wake in the morning and for a moment
see the hexagonal
cage between dimensions,
a realm far
from death, limited
density
circus of troughs and birdseeds
and the constant tock
of time, of uncertain
forever beats like a big black heart
deep in the gory sub-conscious

you see for a second the net, hexagonal and green
a shimmering barrier shining through
from the many densities of sleep
a reminder
that everything you believe
is true
and its much worse than you thought

this cycle is trapped in hypercubes.

Author Bio
* Kealan Coady 1903 -2018 was an Irish writer who lived primarily in Manchester, England. Although generally unrecognised during his lifetime, since his suicide by cop in October 2018, demand for his work has skyrocketed. Not a lot is known about his private life; we know that he was married to noted Swedish Ventriloquist Ingrid Trier and had thirteen children. He is buried in an unmarked grave on the outskirts of Paris.
- - -
* Some or all of this information may be fabricated and cannot be authenticated at this time.

Talking Notebook
by Pasithea Chan

Nights and days are just pages you
Open in me with every step you make.
There's no way of telling if I'll be
Everything you've ever wanted.

Between dreams & nightmares I am an
Open or closed book, an original or a copy depending
On you, but good or bad according to others who
Keep track of the notes you choose to write in me.

Reason isn't my favorite ink for my pages vary
Every now & then in weight & content as per your
Apathy or affection to things that seem to share
Lanes or lores on my lines depending on your vibes.
Imagination and experience colour my pages with your goals.
Trials & losses wash them out or tear them as per your falls.
Yesterday & tomorrow are just my margins or spaces.

Come what may I am you at play.
How many or few are my pages define your
End or longevity for I am your life
Cut short or prolonged whether you
Keep me to yourself or
Share me with others.

(Acrostic spelling: Notebook Reality Checks)

Author Bio
Pasithea Chan is a budding Lebanese Filipino impressionist who enjoys writing poetry in symbolism, laced with philosophy and psychology. She writes in various styles, but prefers pieces that have double meanings to allow the reader to delve deeper into her works.

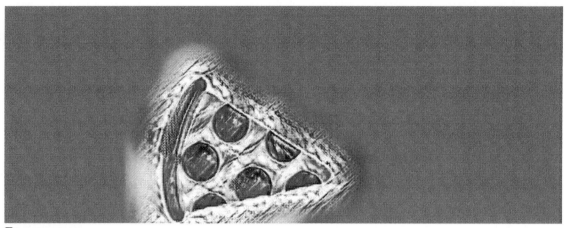

Boomerang
By Victor Nandi

The long ring trailed off leaving the following message on the screen.

Kieron, 28 missed calls.

Deana opened the oven. The aroma of roasted mushrooms and pepperoni filled her nostrils. She pulled out the tray. Chunks of sautéed onions and succulent yellow capsicums teased her from underneath the layer of Mexican cheese. She kept looking at the pizza. It was perfect – just what she had wanted to treat herself with.

She then picked up her handbag and took out a bottle. Removing the cap, she sprinkled the white crystals over the pizza and watched them dissolve in the layers of molten cheese. Deana leant over and took in the sight of the pizza strewn with veggies and meat as she rearranged the toppings to cover any remaining traces of the powder. Her taste buds awoke; her mind revelled in the thought of the slices slipping down her palate; her soul refreshed in the soothing anticipation of atonement for her sins.

She replaced the cap on the bottle of poison and returned it to her handbag.

Her phone rang again.

She picked up the phone and yelled, "what?"

"I want to see you," his voice said from the other end.

"Never again, Kieron. Cheating on him is already too much for me to live with," her voice quivered.

"Just one final time, Deana...please."

30

Deana disconnected the call, despite knowing he meant it. She finished cooking her last supper then leaving it in the switched off oven to keep warm, she picked up the car keys and hurried out of the door.

*

Caindale stepped inside the empty house, an hour later. Sliding the curtains aside, he stood by the window.

The bungalow was located on the top of a hill. Their drawing room offered a beautiful view of the winding road undulating through the scenic landscape down the hill towards the city.

At that moment, Caindale's phone rang. He glanced at the number before answering the unknown caller.

"Hello?"

"Mr. Caindale Oyler?"

"Speaking"

"This is Inspector Jordan. I am afraid your wife, Deana Oyler was involved in an accident."

"WHAT?" Caindale asked. "How is that possible? I spoke to her just..." his words faded into silence.

"Mrs. Oyler was driving towards the city when her car lost balance and toppled over the edge of the road. The paramedics pronounced her dead on the scene. I am so sorry, Mr. Oyler."

Caindale hung up and sighed. Opening the phone's browser settings, he deleted the search history containing *'Tampering with car brakes'*. The corner of his lips curved to form a smile. Caindale had indeed loved her, but could gladly sacrifice everything for his loving Jillianne, even his own wife.

He went to the kitchen, suddenly hungry and wanting to celebrate with a bite to eat. Something was inside the oven, still warm. He opened it. The pizza still looked scrumptious.

Premonition
By Victor Nandi

Lucy looked around, her head twisting from left to right. There were strangers everywhere. Where were her cousins? Where were her friends? The fifteen-year-old girl craned her neck and peered over the ocean of people. She was surrounded by unfamiliar faces and huge frightening rides everywhere.

The giant carousel was whirling like an enormous spinning top. The angry dragon on top of its centre pole, glared up the sky and swayed from one side to another, reminding her of a messenger of the devil nodding at its master.

The passengers shrieked their excitement as the horses at the ends of the carousel's weakly arms tore through the air at breakneck speed.

Lucy pictured those parts suddenly breaking free and scattering everywhere. She envisioned those horses flying through the soft flesh of the surrounding cheerers, limbs and organs of the people smeared on their wooden bodies.

She flinched at the vision and jostled herself away.

"Watch it, girl"

"Hey"

"Are you blind?"

People grumbled as she elbowed through the crowd.

"Where do you think you are going?" Someone grabbed her arm.

Lucy tried to run away, but could not free herself. She turned her head. A yellow-haired man peered at her over his half spectacles. Behind him, stood the heart of the fairground's attraction — the Ferris wheel.

Lucy gaped at the dilapidated pods of the wheel spinning around in enormous vertical circles, like tiny seedcases being lobbed around in huge arcs on slender bars. The hub at the centre of the wheel looked like a massive fist clasping the bars together.

Excited screams and sounds of nervous laughter emanated from the pods, but Lucy couldn't hear them. All she heard was the creaking and squeaking of worn-out hinges and joints. Her mind imagined a narrow crack somewhere along the hub. The next thing she visualised was the whole contraption tumbling down.

She tore away from the man's grasp and fled. But where could she go? There was no place to hide from those horrifying images in her head.

She knew they were all in her mind, which made running away from them impossible. She found herself surrounded by a morass of wounded men and women, as blood appeared to be everywhere.

Lucy ran and stumbled upon a metal lattice. She held onto it with both hands and shook it violently. She squeezed her eyes shut and squealed at the top of her voice, wishing to disappear from the awful scenes around her.

"Hey," a voice interrupted.

Lucy opened her eyes, gasping.

A face had appeared at the other side of the metal lattice. The blood and bodies had gone. There were cheerful faces everywhere bustling about the rides.

"Why are you making a ruckus?" the man asked. "Where are your parents?"

She was unable to reply.

"If you want a ride, you need to pay," the man said. "Screaming about it won't help."

Lucy realised it was a ticket window. *Space Shot* was printed on the board above her in crude handwriting. People were gathering beside her. She moved away and peeked through the crowd. The ride had a seating assembly affixed at the bottom of a long vertical pole which towered over the amusement park. Once the riders were fastened to the chairs, the seating assembly shot up along the wobbly pole at tearing speed. Frenzied screams of riders and loud metallic screeches echoed everywhere as the seats flew into up the rickety spine.

Lucy couldn't stare at it for long. She winced at the images that appeared before her. Her eyes widened and her jaw dropped, as she stood there almost spinning through the frames of her horrifying vision. She turned around and began to run again.

"Get away from here," she bellowed at the people around her. "This place is cursed."

She elbowed her way past the banners reading *Looping Starship*, *Teacups* and *Tumble Bug*.

"The rides are going to crash, people will die," Lucy squeezed through the crowds.

She had no idea where she wanted to go. She just knew she had to escape from the demonic images flurrying in her mind.

People babbled all around her — jubilant faces hustling in queues outside the ticket windows; pleasant-looking couples waiting for their turns on the rides, boisterous boys and girls revelling at dinner tables in the restaurants on both sides of the street. She paid no attention to anyone. Their happy chatter was disturbing to her, their laughter seemed like a nuisance.

Lucy shoved her way to the end of a block of eateries and turned to her right, searching for the exit. Her foot got entangled in something. Unable to hold her balance, she fell.

"Let go off me." she shook her foot and cried.

"Hey, calm down."

Lucy looked up. A young boy was standing over her. His golden hair and light green eyes on a chiselled face would suit a fairy-tale character.

He bent down and held Lucy's foot. "Don't worry, it's just these gas pipes." He was no more than eighteen and his voice had the sensitivity and comfort of a mythical hero.

Lucy kept gazing at him as he held her foot, trying to free it from the mess. She wished for those twisted pipes to cling to her foot harder.

"These damned pipes run everywhere, you know."

Damned? Really?

Very carefully, he released her foot, then stretched out his hand to Lucy.

She held his hand and shook it gently, "I'm Lucy."

"Nice to meet you, Lucy. Umm...can you stand up now?" He looked beautiful when he smiled.

Lucy gave a mesmerised nod and before she knew what was happening, she was walking alongside him.

"I'm Ben."

Wasn't that the most beautiful name she had ever heard?

"This is an old fairground," Ben informed her as they walked. "They have their own gas plant that on side. These pipes supply cooking gas from the central plant to the restaurants."

Lucy went on listening to him, wondering how something so dull could sound so interesting to her.

Ben looked to her for a response. But she just remained, gazing at him without words.

"Why were you running, Lucy?" he asked after studying her a moment.

"I...er...I was lost and I saw..." Her face dropped a little. How could she tell him about what she saw? He would think she was crazy. He wouldn't like her if he thought she was crazy. No one liked crazy.

Ben sensed her discomfort.

"It's fine if you don't want to tell me. I just..."

"No," She didn't want him to think of her as one of those weird girls with silly secrets. "I want to tell you, Ben," she held his hand.

"Do you want to sit somewhere and talk?"

"Yes, but…" she hesitated and looked at the noisy crowd. How could she tell him she wanted to speak to him alone? What would he think of her? She hadn't even known him for ten minutes.

"Relax." He seemed to have read her thoughts. "I know a place."

Ben looked at Lucy, weaving the same magical charm with his smile once again and she could feel her heart pounding.

They walked past the queues at various rides and arcade games while holding hands and talking. The rush of people was huge and their bodies jostled against each other.

They spoke about their hobbies and Lucy diffidently pointed out that she liked to paint.

"That's great. I love cooking," Ben said as they walked. "Do you like steak, Lucy?"

Lucy hated steak but she found herself saying, "yes."

"Great, you can tell me how you like it while I cook." Ben smiled again.

Lucy beamed back.

He took her to a quiet area away from the commotion of rides and gaming arcades. The place stood like the fairground's backyard, away from the crowded alleys.

"That's the powerhouse," Ben pointed to a small grid station surrounded by a raised metal fence. "It supplies electricity to the entire area."

"How do you know so much about this place?" Lucy couldn't help but marvel at his knowledge.

"I work here, Lucy," Ben held her hand tightly as the ground became rocky. "And this is where I come for a quick bite." He stopped outside a small shabby building. It looked like an old storehouse.

"Here?"

Ben opened the door, quickly ushered Lucy inside and closed the door behind them. She glanced behind her as the door shut, doing her best to suppress the cold shiver rushing up her spine.

Just then, Ben turned on the light. Amazed, Lucy saw piles of gas cylinders stacked up throughout the place. At the corner was a coffee machine and a small cabinet for chips and cookies.

"Yes, here" Ben answered sensing Lucy's eyes on the cookies in the cabinet.

Lucy felt her face heat up. How could she have doubted this wonderful guy?

"But when I was talking about food, I was referring to that," Ben pointed to the other corner.

Lucy turned in that direction. A grill and oven stood there.

"It runs on gas." Ben walked over to it and patted it. "And cooks the best steak in town," he added with a wink.

"You run it here?" Lucy glanced over at the stack of cylinders.

"No, my uncle will have me roasted on this grill if I did," Ben replied. "I drag it outside and set it up in the open. He doesn't mind me using the gas line, though."

"But what about the meat? I don't see any here."

Ben studied her for a while, then approached her. "You'll know," he held her hand warmly. "You'll know soon."

Lucy looked up at him, her mouth open and in the next moment found herself lost in his green eyes. The wind sweeping through the windows dishevelled his golden locks in a charming fashion. Suddenly, it all changed. His beautiful face was covered with blood. Flesh hung from his neck, and his shirt was soaking red under a gaping wound. Lucy drew back and closed her eyes.

"Hey," Ben whispered. "Weren't you going to tell me something?"

The demons. The visions.

She opened her eyes and just then, a hand hit on the side of Ben's neck with something sharp. Blood spurted out.

Lucy screamed and closed her eyes. This was no vision and she knew it.

The weapon went in and out of Ben's neck several times. Then the blood-spattered boy collapsed onto the floor.

A few minutes later, there was a deafening explosion and the fairground's central gas chamber erupted in a towering inferno. The grid station followed suit. A devastating fire broke out. It spread through the gas lines and engulfed the entire fairground in a matter of minutes. The rides fell apart with many still sitting in them, the gaming parlours went up in flames and hundreds of people at the restaurants were consumed by the raging fire. Screams erupted out of the flames as people perished under the tumbling bars of steel and burning wood.

Far away, Lucy was walking down the road. Her visions had disappeared. The demons had left, at least for the day. She turned around to look at the fires in the distance. With a sigh, she tied her hair back, using the pointy blood-smeared hair clip and walked away.

Author Bio
Victor Nandi's stories have previously been published by Verdad Magazine and Tiger Shark Magazine. Victor also won a story competition organised by First Naukri, an online job portal in India.

Feelings Are like Seasons
By Ruth O'Reilly

It was so sudden and strange
How the season changed
Winter came
Once again
Way ahead of its time
Now only the ice cold
And uncertainty was real

All that summer sun
Just numb
Should she wait for it to thaw
As she did before
Or set sail
For warmer
Climes?

Never Settled, Never Serious
By Ruth O'Reilly

Like a tourist
Always exploring
Never countries though
No airplanes needed
Just a head up in the clouds
Totally unaware of any pain
That has been caused
There he goes packing that old suitcase again
Suiting himself
Or should that be a trunk?
Elephants sure did have a habit of
Occupying every room
He went into
Maybe one day he'll open a zoo
Just with elephants
His life after all was a circus
And he was a clown
But the lion tamer was always watching

Author Bio
Ruth is a community radio presenter from Manchester. Her love for poetry came from her Mum who would regularly read poetry to her as a child, and her grandad who wrote plays in Ireland and featured in one of the first talking movies to ever be made. At school she wrote the longest stories in English class which other kids enjoyed, but later focused her skills on copy writing.
https://www.writeoutloud.net/blogs/ruthoreilly

Blocked from Heaven's Gate
By Max Northman
(Written in response to being blocked by a religious person on Twitter because my bio contains the Pride flag.)

I wanted to fill your world with love and not with hate-
But through your self-righteous bigotry,
You blocked me from heaven's gate.

You cast the first stone,
As though you have no sin...
Careful with your piety,
Or into hell you'll find yourself in!

Free your heart from all judgement,
And soon your light can truly shine.
You'll prosper more inwardly,
Being closer than ever to The Great Divine.

Lifting up others through kindness, joy and compassion,
Your inner compass guided by a new, selfless goal.
The healing power that comes from acceptance,
Forever keeping your legacy as an example to be retold!

Bio
Max Northman is from the US. He is a writer, husband, fur parent to two rescue dogs and two rescue cats. An unapologetic supporter of Animal Rights, everything from disaster rescue to helping prosecute criminals that abuse, torture, and kill fur babies.

Max's a passion for writing stems from being around all kinds of books as a child. He has several interests ranging from feel-good kid lit to dark and twisted mysteries and thrillers. His goal is to write in a unique voice, regardless of how popular or unpopular that may be. The world has enough faux personalities.
https://maxnorthmanwriterblog.wordpress.com

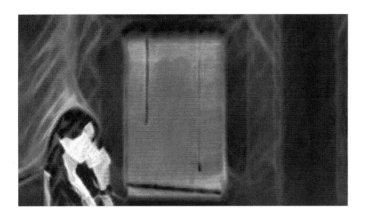

Dark Feelings about Daylight
By Linda Imbler

For those people never charmed
by dawn-to-dark,
who pull the shutters closed.

These lines are written to channel a declaration.

It's okay
if the taste of sunlight
is bitter for you
or if you can't find acceptance
among the tinny voices.

I'm equally perplexed
about those wildly dependent
on the communion of camaraderie.

Like you,
I'm always leaning in the mirror
trying to comprehend why summer's torch
is always blinding.
But I think I never will.

Masks and Mirrors
By Linda Imbler

Hostilities not advertised,
strong sugarcoated resentment,
reflected projections behind
faces always so well disguised.

Subtle insults toward those despised,
vindictive intents kept mirrored
in those hearts competing below
faces always so well disguised.

Somehow cheated and agonized,
fretful, thoughtless pretense cast back,
to be seen from eyes set within
faces always so well disguised.

Feel His Disease
By Linda Imbler

You have always found a way to haunt me,
although yesterday was years ago.
After each night yawns
and midnight has settled into sleep,
you come with your graveyard eyes,
your persistent motif of possessiveness,
trying to gift me once again
with stuffed animals
that shed decades of lint and false fur,
or jewelry that lost its sparkle
and now lays in your hand corroded and corrupt.
All the things that never, ever mattered.

Because all I wanted and needed from you,
were not the darkling, nightmare eyes,
but eyes that really saw me
and reflected the sun.

Author Bio
Linda Imbler is the author of six poetry collections. Since writing her first poem four
years ago, her poetry and short stories have been published in numerous journals. In
addition to putting pen and paper to inventive use, Linda is an avid reader and budding
illustrator. This writer, yoga practitioner and classical guitar player lives in Wichita,
Kansas with her husband, Mike the Luthier, several quite intelligent saltwater fish, and
an ever-growing family of gorgeous guitars.
lindaspoetryblog.blogspot.com

Companion Piece
By Alicia Fitton

In my eyes you are dark leaf and shadow
Bright gilded bronze, messenger and muse
You lead me astray, down paths of sweet sorrow
Tempt me to bargain a life that I'll lose
Muscle and marble, your touch like cold fire
You lead me straight past, my twice daily sin
Mirrored temptation to whet dry desire
The crunch of an apple, the juice on your chin
The vale of my heart, grows ever sickly,
The meadow beyond, remains lush and green
I see our end, arriving so quickly,
The clouds overhead, drop down in between.
I'll gather my thoughts, your heart on my sleeve,
Love me so hard, that I can't hear you leave.

Bio
Alicia Fitton is a performance poet based near Manchester, UK. She writes about lust,
guilt, lies and justified feminist rage. She would like to add more mice and tentacles.
Alicia is a perfectionist who also enjoys dressing up, dancing and playing with swords.
You can read her work at www.stormcloudkittly.com or follow her on Twitter
@aliciamakes

When Rock Was Young
By Gail Scanlon

I remember when Rock was young,
Never mind Elton John.
When you could hear what the singer sang,
And Rock and Roll was fun.

When Elvis swung his pelvis,
To the sound of the Jailhouse Rock.
Girls wore tight tops and poodle skirts
And nobody owned a frock

The guys all had DA haircuts
Though none of them knew what it meant.
Marilyn sang for JFK
And Chanel was her favourite scent.

Our Cliff was the English Elvis
We screamed and cheered and roared
And when he drove that holiday bus
We all wished we were on board

The Shadows did their square dance,
Apache was the tune.
They performed on Ready Steady Go!
Right there, in our living room.

Then all at once it ended.
The King did reign no more.
I remember when it happened,
I was sleeping on a caravan floor.

We were down South on holiday,
Mum, Dad, Sis and me.
Dad went out for a paper,
Brought it back for us to see.

And there is was, on the front page,
The King of Rock had gone,
To that great Vegas in the sky,
The top slot, he had won.

I remember when Rock was young,
When guitar playing was the thing,
When it was cool to be a cat,
And Elvis, was the King.

Chicken Neck
By Elinor Clark

I peeked around the corner, choking on the thick smell of blood. The shuffling sounds of many bodies, the heat from all these creatures crammed in too tightly. Through the semi-darkness, I saw the chickens pressed together.

I slid my gaze away from that writhing mass to the other side of the tall, mesh wire. My eyes fell upon the strange device. It took a second for me to understand what I was seeing. A chicken dangled, hung suspended, grabbed inside the wooden claw. A knife was pressed against its neck, and from the ruby blade blood ran freely, staining feathers, clogging streams trickling down the cadaver.

*

He slipped the necklace around my neck, his fingers clumsily closing the clasp. They lingered there, a bit too long, softly brushing the silky skin. I bit my painted lip, strangely tense, waiting to be released. We had to go. But still he didn't move.

He probed a little, fingers wandering, caught on dimpled mounds of bulging spine, the yielding vales between taut tendons. Awed at the enormity of what lay beneath those hands, that pulsing stem of human life. So soft, so fragile. The thought ran on, sliding, merging, seamlessly transformed into a new idea. He stiffened, repulsed. With one last slippery touch, moved his hand away.

"You've got such a pretty neck," he whispered. I pretended I hadn't heard. In my mind, I saw the chickens.

*

After that day, I stopped wearing necklaces. The chains felt heavy, painfully restrictive against my throat. As soon as I let them fall, I immediately longed to escape their choking grip, to peel off the silver bands and free the clogging flesh.

He noticed. Asked me why I didn't wear the gifts he'd bought. For some reason, I couldn't tell him. It wasn't normal to think like that, to bring to life those dainty strings, transformed to guzzling creatures in my anamorphic lens. I felt them tearing, biting into the diaphanous skin. And now I'd felt it, I couldn't seem to stop feeling it.

He got angry, the next time I was getting ready. Grabbed the box of clanking bands and with a fierce determination, pulled one out. Waved it cruelly, a hypnotic pendulum, swaying back and forth in timed precision. I shuffled away. Not tonight. He didn't stop the swinging.

I stiffened as he pulled me close. Gently, he swept away the hair. It tumbled forward, those glinting locks, freshly brushed. Almost challenging, seeing what I'd do, he laid his hand against my skin. Just kept it there, a heavy clamp. I didn't move. The moment felt too thick, unreal, a rippling stain across this still-life vista. Now we could never rub it out.

A heavy thud. The amber jewel fell hard against my chest. That shining chain wound up around my throat and clicked. There it hung. His hands slipped down. I stepped away.

All night I couldn't ignore the sticky band. The heavy jewel pressed icy lips against my skin, an endless osculation, sucking hard against the flesh. I spun it, tugged it, pulled it hard. But still the clasp would not unseal. Round and round my neck the writhing serpent ran, endless rings around the stretched-out stem.

I had to take it off. I did it subtly, making sure he was not looking. Slowly slipped the burning chain away from flesh and shoved it out of sight, buried in the velvet darkness. But despite all my precautions, I knew he'd seen. I also knew he could not speak, not now at least. The friends were here. Instead he smiled, the curving flesh expanding upwards, thinning in elastic bands as two pink arcs curled close together. He could have been happy, if only the eyes had not betrayed him.

I didn't want the night to end. I kept reviving conversations, manic laughter splurging from the darkness of that gaping void. I felt each time I stretched it wide, I'd go too far and paper skin would slash and tear, a terrifying chasm through my cheeks. No friendly creases embraced by eyes, they bulged and bulged, unblinking orbs. Chickens' eyes.

I slipped into a puerile game, not sure exactly what I meant. I did a dance, the chicken dance, and squawked and flapped and laughed and laughed and folded arms in half to make those crumpled wings. They'd never fly. So soon they'd die. But now they hopped and twirled and staggered round and round that cage, macabre music playing as they danced their final dance; the slaughter dance, the dance of a creature marked for death. The blood surged faster, desperate swells, the heart beat harder, erratic palpitations. Every inch of body so desperately aware it was alive.

At last we left. He held my hand, a suffocating grip, leading as he marched us briskly back. I lingered, slowing, listening as our footsteps slapped across the silent street. Lighter, harder, lighter, harder. We weren't in time.

He unlocked the door, stepping back to let me through. I hovered, uncertain, but stepped inside. Everything felt so wrong. I dumped my coat and wandered up the stairs, my little finger trailing softly on the bannister. I murmured something, far too quiet, my voice escaping in a singsong swell to drift around the house.

I shuffled to our room, not sure what to do. Perched on the bed and stared, shocked, at the gauntness of my face, that strange reflection staring back inside the mirror. It had been too long since I'd properly paused to gaze upon that sheet of glass, since I'd really taken in that small, lined oval. I'd forgotten it could change.

I heard him follow, those footsteps clomping through the room. I didn't move, staring, still as stone. A second later, the footsteps stopped.

In one swift movement, fat flesh clasped together, a clumsy necklace, a thick, distorting collar I was suddenly forced to wear. I couldn't get it off, couldn't slide out of that vice like grip which had me pinned. A dizzying ache began to pulse in numbing waves, sliding through those throbbing points of pressure.

I met his eyes in the reflection, the whole scene smothered in that gorgeous glaze of tragedy. His lips were moving, saying words that didn't reach me. "Pretty neck, pretty neck" I seemed to read. But now I wasn't sure. The world was swaying. He wasn't stopping.

I saw it then, those tiny silver blades, the open scissors innocently strewn upon the painted dresser. Impulse flew. I groped and grabbed and plunged the blade towards his neck.

Silver flashed, the balance tipped and flimsy paper tore apart. A tiny drop at first, a single cerise bud that bloomed and bloomed, the cherry fattening, ripening until it plummeted to the floor. Plop! I plunged again. A scream, a cry, I felt the grip slide free. Stumbled back, the room a sparkling shade of grey.

And as the world began to fade, I saw him there above me. He held his neck, a wounded beast, and anger marred his face. But I was leaving now, I didn't mind. I watched the peeling scarlet gash, entranced to see that flimsy skin make way for leaking blood. That tiny slice expanding out, staining his whole neck in gorgeous red. Just like the chicken, he bled and bled.

Author Bio
Elinor is a recent philosophy graduate hailing from the cold and rainy North of England. She has just started working as a media analyst, and lives in a tiny flat with two ghost housemates, a stick insect and a flourishing mould culture. She writes obsessively; it really is her lifeline and sustaining force. This is her first published story.

The Gift
By Laura Taylor

To have grown without the grain of hate.
To sleep and want to wake before the school day starts.
To finally believe in happy endings, and beginnings,
and later, to know that it wasn't my fault.
To not be the crop she raised from kernel
to a raging field of fire, taking
half a span and passing to extinguish.
To not walk wanting, or wounded through the stubble,
smoke lying low on the horizon,
watching spiral wisps of what could be
and wasn't.

To be raised in a meadow full of buttercups and trust,
and a smile sweetly meant, malice furthest
from the heart as other galaxies to Earth.
To not look for love
in all the thorny places,
from other damaged crops,
recreating origins.
To know enough to realise
that kindness rears the highest yield,
the taller trees, unbent.

What I didn't have myself
I made a present of,
unwrapped and unconditional.
Swaddled her in safe
to grow as tall as trees are meant to grow,
knowing that my heart is hers,
that I am always there
in a meadow
full of buttercups and trust.

Beatitude
By Laura Taylor

We may not light so many fires
but I'll be yours if you'll be mine.
Shallow eyes see lines and grooves
but I see wise and warm and weft,
there's plenty left.
I see proof of life.

Four score and twenty lie between
our bellies, bigger than before,
but soft and more for us to hold.
We fold together, tender in our wrinkled sheets,
and I can see it in your eyes,
we may not light so many fires
but I am yours and you are mine.

We are not bound by gold or ink
but when one sinks, the other lifts,
no one drowns, and when the darkness
comes within, whisper circles on my skin,
let me see how to begin again.

Love is not a cul-de-sac
or paper stained with certainty,
duty-bound or locked in obligation,
but an avenue, a motorway,
an endless path meandering,
holding hands until we reach
our final destination.

Though we sometimes fall and falter,
lose our grip in helter-skelter,
human flaws making diamonds
fall from both our eyes,
salt and glitter, just remember
I am yours and you are mine
and we're alive together,
lighting fires at twilight.

Author Bio

Obsessed with words and language since her early childhood, Laura Taylor believes in the power of poetry as a means by which silent voices speak and hidden ears listen. She is a regular performer at festivals, gigs and fundraisers. Now in her prime, she understands fully the potency of kindness in a world intent on creating division.

She has had two full length poetry collections published by Flapjack Press, and is described by Attila the Stockbroker as "One of the country's finest poets, both on the page and on the stage".

http://www.flapjackpress.co.uk/page32.htm

Mic Drop
By Janey Colbourne

It's a non-stop mic drop situation,
a cause of much deliberation.
At the open mic poetry nights,
there's a need to adjust the microphone height.
It seems we have a broken mic stand.
It just came off in my hand.
Yet again the mic's cut out and dangling,
and we're awfully sick of wrangling
with this wayward piece of kit.
Let's stop before it's all in bits.
As wild and fearsome as a deckchair,
This gear's invoking mild despair.
Can we find a way to prevent this wreck?
There's not much need to have a sound check,
just an estimate of how tall we are.
Perhaps we should stand against the wall?
You can order us all by height,
and spend less time in a technical fight.
All the five-foot twos come forward please.
Still, I'm guessing it's quite likely this blessed thing will seize.
I'm dying to give you some assistance,
when I see the mic stand put up resistance.
You can't attack it like that! It'll just come loose.
You do know that it unscrews? Although not necessarily when you choose.
You may observe with a brief assessment,
it is made for infinite adjustment.
This micro stage is rather small, resembling a ledge.
I'm wincing as I see the feet of the mic stand teetering on the edge.
Don't put it there, oh fuck...
I have to stop myself from jumping up.
Yes, I know I'm a bit of a control freak.
It gets mentioned to me pretty much every week.
As if me sat here, with my jaw clenched, is going make the slightest difference.
You don't need any interference.
I know I have a problem, it's just my fussy brain.
I have a tendency to mumsplain.
It's all going fine, it's a minor issue,
and a source of some amusement.
Even if the whole thing's come undone,
we're all still having fun.
I can see I need to let it go, so,
I'm sorry. I'd better sit down, shut up now, and let you get on with the show.

Over Pain A Void
By Janey Colbourne

In our state of ex-relationship, we paper
over the cracks, bending over backwards
not to offend or fall out, stepping with
care to avoid the gaps, where one of us

might careen into a screaming void of
nightmare memories, of unhealed wounds,
the silent words, that mouth the truth:
what love we had is long since destroyed.

And here remains a shell, as delicate
as fronds of frost against the window pane.
A fragile, intricate design upon
the surface, serves at least to hide the pain.

Don't touch it, for it burns like ice.
The pleasing dance of friendship built on
skirting round the hurt, would all be gone, and
in its place, forsaken demons arise.

Author Bio
Janey Colbourne is a performance poet, nonfiction writer, blogger and musician. She has
been a featured performer at various community and charity events including
Manchester Histories Soapbox, We Shall Overcome, Truth to Power Cafe, and Wigan
Diggers' Festival 2019, and will be a featured performer at That's What She Said,
Manchester in October 2019. Her performances have been described as powerful,
beautiful, courageous, uplifting, fun, open, generous, and 'on fire'. She has been
published in various magazines and is a regular contributor writer for Earth Pathways
Diary. For poetry performance bookings please use the email button on her blog.
heartseer.wordpress.com

Songs of the Starcleaners
By Cathy Bryant

Long ago we swept huts, renewed the rushes
on the packed-earth floor. Then we wiped wood;
next stone.

In offices we learned to use miniature
vacuums on keyboards, special cloths
on monitors.

We sang our songs,
to which no one ever listened,
while we made everything fresher, better.

Later came the starships, and still
we were more cost-effective than robots.
So, we sluiced spacesuits, dusted the bridge,
mopped the holodecks.

When the ultra-rich bought planets,
massive crews of us were flown in
to scrub the seas and tidy continents.
Generations of us lived and died there,
with our own culture, our own art.

Still no one ever listens to us
or our songs. And in ten thousand years,
when the casual owners of the future
survey what they own, they still
will not hear us, will be unable to see us,
however bright the shining light
from the stars we polish.

The Taste of Sock and Rubber
By Cathy Bryant

"Jump!" shout voices. "Jump! Just *do* it!"

They are in front of her, the other children, waiting, expectant, encouraging. And there's an edge of impatience and cruelty too, like cats waiting for fledglings.

"Come *on*, Gemma! We're all waiting!" said one of the big healthy boys.

But I'm so scared, thought Gemma. *I might die. I am terrified.*

A thoughtful parent had cleared the other children off the bouncy castle so that Gemma, too shy to get on it with the careless giggling hordes, could have a go. After all it was her party, her birthday. The other kids were good-natured about it, keen for Gemma to have a fun time, but they wanted her to do it soon, so that they could get back on. These long moments of hesitation felt like selfishness to them.

Gemma could sense this. It had got to the point where they wanted her to do anything at all, bounce confidently or fall weeping on her face. As long as something happened to feed their greed for experience and activity.

I have to do it, thought Gemma miserably, and bent her shaky knees. She leapt gently up, landed and caught the reverberations, but stayed on her feet. More confidently she jumped higher, found a rhythm and started to enjoy the soft floating dance of it. A smile tried itself for size on her face. She could see the other children smile back.

There was something else in their faces, though. *They wanted me to fall*, thought Gemma. They are disappointed. And she bounced around defiantly.

At a signal from one of the parents the whole troop of children swarmed back onto the bouncy castle, whooping and yelling. Suddenly the floor shifted under Gemma's feet and the world became unstable and unsafe again. She tried a weak jump and fell with a cry, a taste of sock and rubber in her mouth. *Don't cry*, she thought, *don't cry*, as she stumbled off the great heaving mass and fastened her new buckle shoes carefully.

And when she was offered lemonade and cake, she was quick to give the appropriate response, wear the correct smile. She wished she could either fit in or else find a quiet place away from the shrieking children.

"It's your special day," her mother beamed.

Author Bio
Cathy Bryant has won 27 literary awards, including the Bulwer-Lytton Fiction Prize and the Wergle Flomp Award for Humorous Poetry. Her work has been published all over the world in such publications as Magma, Dirty Girls, and Stairs and Whispers.

She co-edited the anthologies Best of Manchester Poets vols. 1, 2 and 3. Cathy's own collections are 'Contains Strong Language and Scenes of a Sexual Nature', 'Look at All the Women' and 'Erratics'. Her best-selling book is 'How to Win Writing Competitions'.

Cathy lives in Manchester. She also runs a site of free opportunities for skint writers: www.compsandcalls.com/wp

Printed Words is a non-profit e-zine and print magazine, which currently pays £20 prize money a quarter to one writer. However, by buying a copy rather than choosing the free option, the royalties could be used towards paying more of our writers in the future. The free option will always be available though. We believe good writing should be shared widely.

Other ways to support our writers include visiting the link in their bio, following and liking/sharing their work on social media and buying their published works.

Submission Guidelines
We are looking for:
Poems (up to 50 lines) Creative non-fiction, book reviews or flash fiction (up to 500 words) Short stories (up to 2000 words)
For anything else, ask before submitting.
Deadline: 10th November for December publication.
Send your work **as an attachment** (no identifying details in the document) AND a separate 100-word bio with a link of your choice **in the body of the email**. to contact@amandasteelwriter.com
A maximum of three pieces per quarterly submission period. We accept unpublished and previously published work.

Printed in Poland
by Amazon Fulfillment
Poland Sp. z o.o., Wrocław